MEN
OF
STEWARDSHIP

Dr. Fred L. Hodge, Jr.

ISBN: 978-099817015-2

Library of Congress Control Number: 2017940663

All scriptures are from the King James Version of the Bible.

Knowledge Power Books

A Division of Knowledge Power Communications, Inc.

Valencia, CA 91355

www.knowledgepowerbooks.com

Printed in the United States of America

A BIBLICAL STUDY OF STEWARDSHIP

CONTENTS

INTRODUCTION

As I look back over my upbringing, I can trace many of the attributes that were passed down from my father through his teaching, training, and coaching. He would always promote hard work, in fact, he wanted us to do the job of two men because he said it would guarantee us a job when companies started struggling or downsizing. Well, that is one good reason to be a hard worker but there was also another principle present. I did not know it then, but he was teaching me to be a good steward of another man's possessions. The Bible says it like this - to be faithful in another man's vineyard so that one day God would give me my field to own.

The revelation of Stewardship is critical to every man's success in life; it is the secret to promotion and advancement. We must understand the simple rule, what we have in our hands right now or better yet under our management is enough to prove we can be trusted with more. The management portion of stewardship is key to elevation, promotion, and increase. How you treat, respect, and care for what you have been entrusted with will bring with it recognition, acknowledgment, and reward. These practices are all connected and give insight into how duplication, elevation, and manifestation takes place. The Bible quote is "Whatever good thing we do for others, God will cause the same to happen to us." This principle helps us to understand you cannot loose in the position of serving others. Supposing they are "just" and "fair" in returning correct reciprocation for your great efforts in a natural way or not, your heavenly Father will spiritually acknowledge, recognize, and reward your efforts.

Opportunity begins to align itself with your life. Another principle that supports the Stewardship role in a man's life is the principle of sowing and reaping. Sowing and reaping was a law set up in the time of Noah after the flood. It is a spiritual and natural law that cannot be denied.

Scriptures are the bedrock of human existence once God puts his Word on it nothing can reverse or change it.

Galatians 6:7 - *Be not deceived; God is not mocked: for whatsoever a man soweth, that shall he also reap. This can be negative or positive; the emphasis is you get back what you put in. As a man, I cannot complain or murmur about another man's blessing, since we all have opportunities to prove we are worthy of promotion and increase.*

According to scriptural documentation every human being is born into the earth without natural resources and consequently will leave everything behind he has accumulated for others to inherit or enjoy when he makes his exit from the earth. In making the transition from earth to heaven men will leave everything they have collected in this natural life behind them. The law of possession is restricted to lifespan, what you accomplish and accumulate in this natural life is only useful in this natural life. Everything you experience in earth is only for a time. You only manage it while you are here, then you must release it when you make your exit out of this life.

When we understand the position of a Steward it takes away the element of jealousy and competition. A man can only have what his faith can produce; therefore, he is not justified in his anger against another man for his success. We are all given a measure of faith; it becomes stronger and more powerful with use. Your faith as a steward is critical to promotion and possession of the promises given to every man by God. Put your faith to work, and what seems to be impossible becomes possible; what seems to be difficult moments, become defining moments of victory and breakthrough. The Word of God says in **Ephesians 2:10 -** *God has made us what we are in Christ Jesus, God made us to do good works, which God planned in advance for us to live our lives doing.* (NCV)

Gentlemen, welcome to the life of the Steward; you are God's workman created to do good works.

WHAT IS A STEWARD?

The definition of Steward is as follows:

1. A house distributor, otherwise known as manager or overseer;

2. A Steward can also be an employee in that capacity;

3. Can also be interpreted a fiscal agent such as a treasurer;

4. Figuratively, a preacher of the Gospel; King James defines him as a Chamberlain, a Governor, or a Steward.

Wisdom Keys

The power to define is the power to change or influence destiny. My capacity to understand something, how it works, how it produces, how it is activated, will elevate my potential to operate on a higher scale of productivity.

Destiny is not automatic it is the result of the choices you willfully make for your life. Purpose and destiny are tied together by choices. If we choose the plan God has for our lives and fulfill his divine purpose, we end up with that as our destiny. If we make our own plans and choose a different path we end up with the results of that effort as our destiny.

The problem with following our own plan, and not following God's plan is that He has designed a certain future to accompany the fulfilment of His purposes for us, and choosing our own plan will forfeit the results He intended for us to experience. If we insist on following our own ambition,

NOTES

NOTES

we will be limited to what our intellect, our human will, and our affiliation with others can produce; which will cause us to miss out on what was possible through faith in God, who is our divine architect.

Important terms to know about being a Steward:

He is a manager – one who handles, controls or directs a business or other enterprise; one who controls resources and expenditures of a household, and one who is in charge of the training and performance of an athlete or a team.

He is a fiscal agent – someone who oversees finances for an organization.

He is a preacher – one who preaches, and publicly proclaims the Gospel for an occupation. Preach means to proclaim or put forth in a sermon; to advance, especially to urge acceptance of or compliance with; to deliver (a sermon, a message, instruction).

Every head-of-household is commissioned to teach his family the Word of God.

He is a chamberlain – an officer who manages the household of a sovereign or noble; a chief steward; a high-ranking official in various royal courts.

He is a governor – a person who governs, an official appointed to govern territory; the manger or administrator of an organization, business or institution. That covers family life as well. Singles are also required to institute governments over themselves.

He is a steward – one who manages another's property finances or other affairs. One who is in charge of the household affairs of a large estate, a club, hotel or resort.

In reading the definitions of Stewardship we see the importance and the value this position holds. We see, it is a position of responsibility and accountability. The position of a Steward demands certain qualifications such as faithfulness, loyalty, commitment, and persistence; without these qualities, a person would fail to fulfill the Stewardship position.

REVIEW AND DISCUSSION FOR SECTION ONE

WHAT IS A STEWARD?

Why is the power to define so powerful?

- The power to define is the _____ to change or _____ destiny. My capacity to understand something, how it works, how it produces, how it is activated, will elevate my potential to operate on a higher scale of productivity.

Is destiny guaranteed?

- Destiny is not automatic. It is the result of the _____ you willfully make for your life.

- If we choose the plan _____ has for our lives and fulfill His divine _____, we end up with that as our _____.

- If we make our _____ plans and choose a different path, we end up with the _____ of that effort as our _____.

How are destiny and purpose tied together?

- Purpose and destiny are tied together by _____.

What is the problem with making my own plan for my life?

It forfeits _____results

- The problem with following our own plan and not following God's plan is that He has designed a certain future to accompany the fulfilment of His purposes for us, and choosing our own plan will forfeit the results He intended for us to experience.

They promote _____

- If we insist on following our own ambition, we will be limited to what our intellect, our human will, and our affiliation with others can produce, which will cause

NOTES

us to miss out on what was possible through faith in God, who is our divine architect.

What is a steward and how does that apply to us as men today?

a. _____

b. _____

c. _____

d. _____

SECTION TWO

BIBLICAL STEWARDSHIP

Since the Bible is our text for this subject, let's read some verses that enlighten us on the principles of Stewardship.

1 Corinthians 4:1 - *Let a man so account of us as of the ministers of Christ and stewards of the mysteries of God, 2 moreover it is required in stewards that a man be found faithful.*

The first priority trait of a Steward is to be found faithful. To be Faithful is defined as trustworthy, sure, and true; it is also defined with the terms *believe* and *believing*, which denotes being a believer.

Faithfulness is a requirement that all stewards must possess as they function in life. Faithfulness is the criteria by which a man's character is measured and whereupon certain possibilities are presented to him. Without faithfulness, you rob yourself of future opportunities.

Jesus taught on the faithful Steward:

Luke 16:10 - *He that is faithful in that which is least is faithful also in much: and he that is unjust in the least is unjust also in much. 11 If therefore ye have not been faithful in the unrighteous mammon, who will commit to your trust the true riches? 12 And if ye have not been faithful in that which is another man's, who shall give you that which is your own? 13 No servant can serve two masters: for either he will hate the one, and love the other; or else he will hold to the one, and despise the other. Ye cannot serve God and mammon. KJV*

The priority principle in Luke is the same as the one found in

1 Corinthians 4:2 - *which is faithfulness, in fact the virtue of faithfulness defines a man's character and trustworthiness. If he is faithful in little things, that same man will be found to be faithful in the larger areas of life. So faithfulness is the area of conquest for every man. Whatever you are given to steward, it is critical you are faithful over it until the end. Your character is judged by it, and your future is measured by it.*

No man can expect promotion in his future without being faithful in his present.

Where you are in life is a product of yesterday's performance. The effort you put forth, the integrity you characterized, and the faithfulness exemplified are all qualities that get recognition, acknowledgment, and reward. These qualities qualify you for future opportunities.

NOTES

REVIEW AND DISCUSSION FOR SECTION TWO

BIBLICAL STEWARDSHIP

What does the Bible say is the priority requirement for Stewards?

- Moreover, it is required in Stewards that a man be found _____.

- The first _____ trait of a Steward is to be found faithful.

- To be *faithful* is defined as _____, _____, and _____.

- It is also defined with the terms _____ and _____, which denotes being a believer.

Is it necessary to practice the virtue of faithfulness?

- Faithfulness is a _____that all Stewards must possess as they function in life.

- Faithfulness is the criteria by which a man's _____ is measured and whereupon certain _____ are presented to him.

- Without _____, you rob yourself of future opportunities.

What is the area of conquest for every man?

- Faithfulness is the area of _____ for every man.

- The virtue of faithfulness defines a man's character and _____.

- If he is faithful in _____ things, that same man will be found to be faithful in the _____ areas of life.

- Whatever you are given to Steward, it is critical you are _____ over it until the _____.

- Your character is _____ by it and your future is _____ by it.

NOTES

SECTION THREE

THE REVELATION OF STEWARDSHIP LIMITATION

Luke 16:10 - *He who is faithful in a very little thing is faithful also in much and he who is dishonest and unjust in a very little thing is dishonest and unjust in much. 11 Therefore if you have not been faithful in the case of unrighteous mammon, which is deceitful riches, money possessions, who will entrust to you the true riches? 12 And if you have not proved faithful in that which belongs to another whether it is God or man, who will give you that which is your own that is the true riches? 13 No servant is able to serve two masters; for either he will hate the one and love the other or he will stand by and be devoted to the one and despise the other. You cannot serve God and mammon, which are riches or anything in which you trust and on which you rely.* (AMP)

This passage also reveals a steward limitation. A Steward cannot serve two masters faithfully. He will love one and hate the other, and he will hold to the one, and despise the other. It is impossible to have split loyalties when it comes to those who have positions of power and authority in our lives. I call these priority relationships. The example of a priority relationship would be **work-related**, hired by a company to do a specific job dedicating 40 hours a week to meet the requirements. **Family-related** such as a spousal situation that commands faithfulness to one person in regards to intimacy, provision, esteem, and respect. **Kingdom-related** where choices must be made concerning who I worship, where I serve, and where I sow.

NOTES

NOTES

The revelation of Stewardship limitation

The limitation is not one of skill, ability, or capacity, but one of attachment, connection, and emotional ties. These emotional components will influence a person's motivation and their performance levels. If you are in conflict with your loyalties, then you will not be motivated to use your gifts, talents, and skill sets to help or assist your priority relationships. The person challenging that relationship will cause an emotional shift; therefore, limiting a person's output in his performance. Such as when a man starts creating a soul-tie outside his marriage. This new relationship becomes a challenge because it will make demands upon him that will rob the relationship he has with his wife. He becomes less motivated to be with his wife, to serve his wife, and to be intimate with his wife. His focus shifts to where his attention is placed, and attachments of affection are created, and his spiritual covenant with his wife is violated. Though he keeps his affair a secret, all will feel the spiritual violation. The wife will sense a change in loyalty, a shift in her spouse's attention, affection, and affirmation. She can tell he is no longer listening to her, and that she is not his priority; and excuses take the place of exceptional performance. She notices a subtle change in his advances for intimacy, his sex pattern changes, and then subtle criticisms of his spouse's performances becomes the priority of their conversations.

We were created and designed to respect, honor, and cherish relational attachment. Human beings crave acceptance and approval from their peers, sometimes to the degree of compromising who they are, and what they stand for in life. It is important to choose wisely when forming associations. The choice aspect of free *will* should be governed by your beliefs, and convictions that are founded in the truth of God's Word. In other words, no matter how you admire or respect a person, if their value system is opposite to yours, and contradicts your beliefs, then that particular person is not an option for a relationship. You can work with them or work for them but not make a covenant with them. You can be cordial and kind but not connected. Soul-ties will create loyalties that even a Christian will protect, despite what the Bible tells us, *"Be not unequally yoked with unbelievers"*.

REVIEW AND DISCUSSION FOR SECTION THREE

THE REVELATION OF STEWARDSHIP LIMITATION

What are Stewardship limitations?

- A Steward cannot _____ two _____ faithfully.

Why can't a man split his loyalties?

- He will _____ one and _____ the other.

- He will _____ to the one and _____ the other.

- It is impossible to have split _____ when it comes to those who have _____ of power and authority in our lives. I call these _____ relationships.

What are some examples of priority relationships?

The example of a priority relationship would be:

1. _____, hired by a company to do a specific job, dedicating 40 hours a week to meet the requirements.

2. _____, such as a spousal situation that commands faithfulness to one person in regards to intimacy, provision, esteem, and respect.

3. _____, where choices must be made concerning who I worship, where I serve, and where I sow.

Can we define these limitations?

- The limitation is not one of skill, ability, or capacity, but one of _____, _____, and _____ ties.

- These emotional components will influence a person's _____ and their _____ levels.

NOTES

- If you are in conflict with your _____, then you will not be _____ to use your gifts, talents, and skill sets to _____ or _____ your priority relationships.

- The person challenging that relationship will cause an _____ shift; therefore, limiting a person's _____ in his performance.

How important are associations in our lives?

- We were created and designed to _____, _____, and _____relational attachment.

- Human beings crave _____ and _____ from their peers; sometimes to the degree of _____ who they are and what they stand for in life.

- It is important to choose _____ when _____ associations.

What is the criteria for making good choices?

- The choice aspect of free will should be governed by your _____ and _____ that are founded in the truth of God's Word.

- In other words, no matter how you admire or respect a person, if their _____ system is opposite to yours and _____ your beliefs, then that particular person is not an option for a _____.

- You can work with them or work for them, but not make a _____ with them.

- You can be cordial and kind, but not _____. Soul-ties will create _____ that even a Christian will _____ despite what the Bible tells us, *"Be not unequally yoked with unbelievers"*.

SECTION FOUR

STEWARDSHIP ACCOUNTABILITY

God uses this principle of the Steward in explaining how Kingdom works. In the Kingdom of God, it is very clear that we are given responsibilities with accountability. Your work is not just trusted but also inspected; it must meet the criteria of God's requirements. Both Cain and Abel brought an offering to the Lord, but God rejected Cain's offering. **_The quality of his gift reflected the condition of his heart._** It was inspected and rejected. God is a God of order. He creates everything with a purpose and He sets in place creative mandates that promote fulfillment and satisfaction.

Luke 12:42 - _And the Lord said, who then is that faithful and wise steward, whom his lord shall make ruler over his household, to give them their portion of meat in due season? 43 Blessed is that servant, whom his lord when he cometh shall find so doing. 44 Of a truth I say unto you, that he will make him ruler over all that he hath. 45 But and if that servant say in his heart, my lord delayeth his coming; and shall begin to beat the menservants and maidens, and to eat and drink, and to be drunken; 46 The lord of that servant will come in a day when he looketh not for him, and at an hour when he is not aware, and will cut him in sunder, and will appoint him his portion with the unbelievers. 47 And that servant, which knew his lord's will, and prepared not himself, neither did according to his will, shall be beaten with many stripes. 48 But he that knew not, and did commit things worthy of stripes, shall be beaten with few stripes. For unto whomsoever much is given, of him shall much be_

NOTES

required: and to whom men have committed much, of him they will ask the more. (KJV)

This points out that a Steward should not only be faithful, but wise. The Gospel of Saint Luke also speaks of elevation for the Steward who has been faithful; *he is promoted not just in the house but ruler over all that the master has*.

When you are a good Steward, you not only gain attention and acknowledgement, but you also gain access. The more dedicated the Steward, the greater the access into his master's things. You may start out in one area of responsibility, but through wise practices and faithfulness, the steward can be elevated to a greater portion of the estate.

NOTES

NOTES

REVIEW AND DISCUSSION FOR SECTION FOUR

STEWARDSHIP ACCOUNTABILITY

Are we accountable for our actions?

- In the Kingdom of God, it is very clear that we are given _____ with _____.

As a Steward, why is my work inspected?

- Your work is not just _____ but also _____; it must meet the criteria of God's requirements.

- Both Cain and Abel brought an offering to the Lord, but God _____ Cain's offering. The quality of his gift reflected the _____ of his heart, and it was _____ and _____.

- God is a God of _____. He creates everything with a _____ and sets in place creative mandates that promote fulfillment and satisfaction.

What do I gain for being a good Steward?

- When you are a good Steward, you not only gain _____ and _____, but you also gain _____.

- The more _____ the Steward, the _____ the _____ into his master's things.

- You may start out in one area of _____, but through wise _____ and _____, the Steward can be _____ to a greater portion of the estate.

SECTION FIVE

STEWARDSHIP REWARD

Reward of the Steward

Matthew 25:14 - *Again, the Kingdom of Heaven can be illustrated by the story of a man going on a long trip. He called together his servants and entrusted his money to them while he was gone. 15 He gave five bags of silver to one, two bags of silver to another, and one bag of silver to the last—dividing it in proportion to their abilities. He then left on his trip. 16 "The servant who received the five bags of silver began to invest the money and earned five more. 17 The servant with two bags of silver also went to work and earned two more. 18 But the servant who received the one bag of silver dug a hole in the ground and hid the master's money. 19 "After a long time their master returned from his trip and called them to give an account of how they had used his money. 20 The servant to whom he had entrusted the five bags of silver came forward with five more and said, 'Master, you gave me five bags of silver to invest, and I have earned five more.' 21 "The master was full of praise. 'Well done, my good and faithful servant. You have been faithful in handling this small amount, so now I will give you many more responsibilities. Let's celebrate together!' 22 "The servant who had received the two bags of silver came forward and said, 'Master, you gave me two bags of silver to invest, and I have earned two more.' 23 "The master said, 'Well done, my good and faithful servant. You have been faithful in handling this small amount, so now I will give you many more responsibilities. Let's celebrate together!' 24 "Then the servant with the one bag of silver came and said, 'Master, I knew you were a harsh man, harvesting crops you didn't plant and gathering crops you didn't cultivate. 25 I was afraid I would lose your money, so I hid it in the earth. Look, here is your money back.'*

26 "But the master replied, 'you wicked and lazy servant! If you knew I harvested crops I didn't plant and gathered crops I didn't cultivate, 27 why didn't you deposit my money in the bank? At least I could have gotten some interest on it.' 28 "Then he ordered, 'Take the money from this servant, and give it to the one with the ten bags of silver. 29 To those who use well what they are given, even more will be given, and they will have abundance. But from those who do nothing, even what little they have will be taken away. 30 Now throw this useless servant into outer darkness, where there will be weeping and gnashing of teeth. (NLT)

First Concept:

Ownership versus Stewardship

First, let's break down the story and deal with each concept as it comes up. The first concept is knowing you are a Steward to the One who created you. **Psalm 100:3** says, *Know that the Lord, He is God; it is He who has made us, and not we ourselves; we are His people and the sheep of His pasture.* (NKJV)

We know that Scripture says that all things belong to God and He gives man the authority to care and nurture the things He has created. From the beginning, even in the Garden of Eden, man was given the responsibility for the Garden to dress it and to keep it. So, the critical perspective that influences the heart of the Steward is this, all things belong to God who has given us the privilege of managing, caring for, and enjoying the things He has created. Stewardship is a privilege and not an entitlement. Your purpose for living is to please God with your Stewardship.

Second Concept:

Assessment of Ability

The distribution of goods is based on the perception of the owner. He assesses the capability of each Steward and distributes according to his ability to manage, care for, and increase the owner's goods. You and I must reconcile the fact that others have more ability than we do and some have less ability than we do. We cannot allow ourselves to get into a mindset of competition and jealousy because someone has more than us. Remember, the assessment revealed the

NOTES

NOTES

ability of each Steward. When you are given more than you can handle, you lose it. The secret to elevation is to be *fixed, focused,* and *functioning* in the measure of responsibility you have in life. You increase what is in your hand by way of use. When you are more *talk* than *action,* you fail to grow, and there is no multiplication or increase.

Third Concept:

When Responsibility is given, Accountability is required.

The owner will always return for accountability. He will require an audit of your work to see if you respected the privilege of Stewardship. His audit will include the assessment of faithfulness in the Steward. We see in the story, the owner promoted those who used the ability to increase what was given to them. Because of their faithfulness to manage, care for, and increase his goods, they were given more to manage. Every Steward who used his ability to increase what he was given received a promotion and reward, but the steward who hid his Lord's goods and returned his Stewardship without increase was dishonored. He even lost what was given to him; it was taken from him and given to the one with ten talents. When you don't *use* what you have, you *lose* what you have. The saying "Use it or Lose it" really does apply here.

Fourth Concept:

Condition of the Steward's heart

The two Stewards who took the responsibility as a privilege were promoted, but the one who despised using his ability for another man's work lost what he was given. Notice the other two men were not treated with equality. They were entrusted with the measure of their ability. Each one produced results according to his own ability. One of the secrets to maximum effort is to have a correct estimation of oneself. Not to think more highly than one should think. When you self-elevate in your mind based on emotional reasoning and not results, you keep yourself in a state of deception, which leads to other things. It is critical for the Steward that he starts with what he is given. Through proper management, he will then increase his skill and prove his character.

Fifth Concept:

Faithfulness is a Requirement

Faithfulness determines whether you are profitable or unprofitable in God's Kingdom. Those that have faithfulness will always be given more. The principle of faithfulness is where abundance is produced with the continual use of personal ability, coupled with faith to increase Kingdom fruit. In the story, we see different elements practiced by the two productive Stewards. The first being faith. They believed the word of the owner; so faith was the foundation for their motivation to fulfill their assignment. The good Stewards worked diligently with what was given to them and produced increase. Notice the persistence, when the owner returned, they were still putting forth effort to achieve their highest potential. Attitude is significant because it revealed their choice to serve and not to sit. A *doing* person will always achieve more than a *sitting* person. People like to sit on the throne of criticism, comparison, and compromise, instead of standing on the pillar of hard work, honor, honesty and humility. In today's secular society, it is about entitlement or intelligence, and not the relevance of integrity and character content. Let me conclude by saying this, we must be *doers* of the Word and not just *hearers* only.

Sixth Concept:

Stewardship

Stewardship is the true basis for all mentorship to take place. When I am not in the place of a Steward, I have no proof of a right-now commitment to my appointment. I only have the argument of a dusty résumé that I have put away, which is guarded by my ego and verified through my pride.

1) **Stewardship puts me in a place to be trusted.**

2) **Stewardship puts me in a place to be tested – no promotion without testing.**

3) **Stewardship puts me in a place to be taught – teaching comes with communication, observation, and participation.**

NOTES

NOTES

_____
_____
_____
_____
_____
_____
_____
_____
_____
_____
_____
_____
_____
_____
_____
_____
_____
_____
_____
_____
_____
_____
_____
_____
_____
_____
_____

- Communication - You can learn by hearing instruction.

- Observation - You can learn by seeing the example.

- Participation - You can learn by hands-on involvement.

REVIEW AND DISCUSSION FOR SECTION FIVE

STEWARDSHIP REWARD

What is the critical perspective that influences the heart of the Steward?

- We know that Scripture says that all things belong to God and He gives man the _____ to _____ and _____ the things He has created.

- From the beginning, even in the Garden of Eden, man was given the _____ for the Garden to dress it and to keep it.

- The critical perspective that _____ the heart of the Steward is this - all things belong to _____ who has given us the _____ of _____, caring for, and enjoying the things He has created.

- Stewardship is a _____ and not an _____.

- Your _____ for _____ is to _____ God with your _____.

How does God distribute fairly?

- The distribution of goods is based on the _____ of the _____.

- He _____ the capability of each Steward and _____ according to the Steward's _____ to manage, care for, and _____ the owner's goods.

- You and I must reconcile the fact that some may have more _____ than we do and some may have less _____ than we do.

- We cannot allow ourselves to get into a_____ of _____ and _____ because someone has more than we have in life.

NOTES

- Remember, the _____ revealed the _____ of each Steward.
- When you are given _____ than you can _____, you _____ it.

What is the secret to promotion?

- The secret to elevation is to be _____, _____ and _____ in the measure of responsibility you have.
- You _____ what is in your hand by way of _____.
- When you are more _____ than _____ you fail to _____ and there is no multiplication or increase.

Use concepts 3-6 as discussions points.

They are rich with revelation.

SECTION SIX

THE FIRST STEWARD WAS ADAM

Adam the first Steward

To understand our role in Stewardship we must go back to creation where everything began. Genesis, the book of beginnings, documents many principles, which are called the law of first mention. You can define the importance of a purpose or function by how it's used in the creative order of God. Let's read through the creative order and discover our place as Stewards in the design of God.

Genesis 2:1 - *Thus the heavens and the earth were finished, and all the host of them. 2 And on the seventh day God ended his work which he had made; and he rested on the seventh day from all his work which he had made. 3 And God blessed the seventh day, and sanctified it: because that in it he had rested from all his work which God created and made. 4 These are the generations of the heavens and of the earth when they were created, in the day that the LORD God made the earth and the heavens, 5 And every plant of the field before it was in the earth, and every herb of the field before it grew: for the LORD God had not caused it to rain upon the earth, and there was not a man to till the ground.6 But there went up a mist from the earth, and watered the whole face of the ground. 7 And the LORD God formed man of the dust of the ground, and breathed into his nostrils the breath of life; and man became a living soul. 8 And the LORD God planted a garden eastward in Eden; and there he put the man whom he had formed. 9 And out of the ground made the LORD God to grow every tree that is pleasant to the sight, and* *good for food; the tree of life also in the midst of the garden, and the tree of knowledge of good and evil. 10 And a river went out of Eden to water the garden; and from thence it was parted, and became into four heads.* (KJV)

We see in Genesis chapter two the order of the creative process. Since all natural things flow from a spiritual source, God finishes his work spiritually first then manifests that work in a physical reality. This is why He knows the end from the beginning. This is why the Scripture says all things were finished from the foundation of the world. This is why we can have this confidence in His plan for our lives. Everything about us has been written before our parents gave birth to us. Your life is hidden together with Christ in God. God does all things well so there is no need to worry about provision, protection, or peace.

The first habitat of man reveals how God premeditated His support and supply for Adam. When we look at the nature of God, He never creates without purpose and He never creates without support. Verse eight says he planted a garden eastward in Eden, and there put the man who he had formed. He created a safe haven to sustain the man, a supportive environment that nurtured him. The Father creates every tree that is pleasant to the sight and good for food. Then He creates the tree of life in the midst of the garden and the tree of knowledge of good and evil, all in the garden where man lived. Then God gives Adam the responsibility of Stewardship.

The responsibility of man:

Genesis 2:15 - *And the LORD God took the man, and put him into the garden of Eden to dress it and to keep it. 16 And the LORD God commanded the man, saying, of every tree of the garden thou mayest freely eat: 17 But of the tree of the knowledge of good and evil, thou shalt not eat of it: for in the day that thou eatest thereof thou shalt surely die.* (KJV)

Responsibilities of the Steward of the house:

In this passage we see God took the man and put him into the Garden of Eden and gave him responsibility. You are to dress it and you are to keep it. Every man is the guardian of his garden and held responsible for what goes on there.

NOTES

NOTES

We see the first mention of Stewardship of man:

You are to dress the garden. *Dress it* means to work to serve, to till, to labor over. The King James Version defines it this way: to set at work, be wrought, and worshipper.

Define *work* – a physical or mental effort or activity directed toward the production or accomplishment of something; a job or employment; a trade profession or other means of livelihood. The definition is so powerful. It emphatically tells us that God made us and gave us a job. He spiritually employed us. He made us and put us to work in His Kingdom.

The word *work* also means something that one is doing, making, or performing especially as an occupation or undertaking; a duty of occupation or undertaking a duty or task.

Define *wrought* – a past tense and a past participle of work, put together, create, or shape by hammering with tools used chiefly of metal or metalwork; made delicately or elaborately.

So the word *wrought* gives us another view of being a steward. My work gives shape to what I am responsible for in life. I have the ability to make it elaborate, beautiful, or soft and delicate. I create with the substance I have been given. My marriage can be something of beauty when I steward it properly. The lives of my children are delicate and innocent and must be handled with care if they are to grow into well-balanced, healthy adults. The touch of a father is critical in shaping the child's identity, security, and courage. Men, your Stewardship over your families is critical to their growth, their success, their joy, and happiness. This principle applies to all other areas of your life, your contribution to God's Kingdom, your contribution to community, and your career right down to hobbies and past times. These outcomes are the product of your understanding, the result of your effort, the commitment to responsibility, and the passion you have for your work. I am a steward over my family. This is where I must do my best work.

Define *worshipper* – the reverent love and devotion accorded a deity or an idol or a sacred object; the ceremonies, prayers, or other religious forms by which this love is expressed; ardent devotion, adoration; to honor and love a deity; to regard with ardent or adoring esteem or devotion; to revere; to perform an act of worship.

When a man dresses his garden, it is an act of worship to the one who entrusted him with it. The man is not the owner of the garden, but the dresser of the garden. He sculptures it, he prunes it, he shapes it according to his vision and design, and keeping in mind he is managing something that belongs to another. When God created the Garden, it was to be Adam's habitat, the place of loving, living, and learning. Everything he needed was provided here and his care, respect, and honor for what he was given became an act of his worship to God.

First Remember, MOVE Men, your Stewardship is not only a responsibility, but also a show of worship to the One who entrusted you with everything you have. So when you love your wife and raise a family, when you go to work to provide a life for them, when you take your family to church, it is all considered a part of your worship to the Lord.

Second responsibility – to keep it

Jesus teaches that as a Steward, you must have a conviction that you will be accountable for what you are responsible for. Your work will be inspected so one must be wise in his approach to what he has been entrusted with.

Matthew 24:43 - *But know this, that if the good man of the house had known in what watch the thief would come, he would have watched, and would not have suffered his house to be broken up. 44 Therefore be ye also ready: for in such an hour as ye think not the Son of man cometh. 45 Who then is a faithful and wise servant, whom his lord hath made ruler over his household, to give them meat in due season? 46 Blessed is that servant, whom his lord when he cometh shall find so doing. 47 Verily I say unto you, that he shall make him ruler over all his goods. 48 But and if that evil servant shall say in his heart, my lord delayeth his coming; 49 And shall begin to smite his fellow servant's, and to eat and drink with the drunken; 50 The lord of that servant shall come in a day when he looketh not for him, and in an hour that he is not aware of, 51 And shall cut him asunder, and appoint him his portion with the hypocrites: there shall be weeping and gnashing of teeth.* (KJV)

Define *to keep it* - to hedge about, to guard; generally to protect, attend to.

NOTES

NOTES

King James defines it like this - be circumspect, take heed, keep, mark, look narrowly, observe, preserve, regard, reserve, save self; sure; wait for; watchman.

This is quite a definition of man's function to observe, preserve, regard, reserve, and to be a watchman.

The watchman is a primary function of the man. It is defined like this: to lean forward, to peer into the distance, to observe, and to await.

Let's go through these definitions, being they are the attributes of a Steward.

The word *circumspect* means to be prudent, careful, judicial, and focused along with other words that give us the term *balanced*. In order to be *balanced*, a man must be a student and a teacher. You must never get to the place where you think of yourself as arrived, all knowing, having all wisdom, in need of no one or nothing to assist you. Even after God's creation of Adam, He looked at His work and said, "It is not good that man should be alone. I will make a helpmate just for him."

MOVE Men, to keep balance, you must have a Mentor, someone you look up to and get wisdom and instruction from, a man of wisdom to impart into your life who can make corrections and adjustments in your life. You must also have a Main-Key Man, a friend that you walk with in life, another man who has the same experiences and responsibilities you have; the Bible says, a brother whom you can depend upon for sharpening. Iron sharpens Iron. Then you need a Mentee, someone who you are reaching out to as a teacher and a guide. When you are sowing into someone else's life, you are completing the cycle of student/teacher that keeps you balanced. This kind of flow keeps revelation coming in and going out. The more you teach what you know the greater your capacity becomes for learning. One of the Achilles heels for men is the misunderstanding of humility and submission. Humility is not a sign of weakness, but a sign of honor. You have the right perspective of yourself and pride cannot override possible opportunities. And submission is not giving away your power, but the creation of a bridge to greater power. Submission and humility are the keys to grace transfer. You can only acquire what you are willing to submit to as a covering. The difference between a *cap* and a *covering* needs to be explained. A *cap* is there to keep things in, to contain and not allow access out. A *covering* is there to draw out of you what is in you. A covering creates an environment of learning, growing, and maturing as well as activation and manifestation of gifts and talents.

Remember, MOVE Men, one of your most valuable assets for balance is submission. When you have no source upstream, you are fishing from a dead sea. The lake must have a source from upstream as well as an outlet downstream. Without these, no new things can get in and no old things can get out. This is an indication of stagnation, which produces frustration in a man's life. Growth and change are products of new knowledge. When we are not learning, we are not growing. The Bible says, *My people perish for a lack of knowledge or because they have rejected knowledge.* We can only grow to the level of what we know. Jesus said, *"And you shall know the truth and the truth you know shall set you free."* So, it is not just knowing a lot of things, but understanding the knowledge you have and applying it. He also said, "Continue in my Word and you shall be my disciples indeed." The focus word being *continue.* We must have a hunger and thirst to learn. There is a biblical promise that goes along with a passion to learn. He that hungers and thirsts for righteousness shall be filled. If the passion for learning is absent, we begin to lose ground; instead of being progressive we become regressive going backwards.

We were made to be spiritually progressive, ever learning, living, and loving to maintain soundness of mind and preservation of soul. We were created to be achievers, producers, providers, and protectors. That is the reason we have the stronger bodies and we were given a system of focus that brings stability and security to the family. Our families can trust us to keep them safe; they can rely upon us to provide for their needs on a regular basis and be their foundation to stand on throughout life.

Now that we have an understanding of Stewardship, let's take its primary quality and study it. That quality is *faithfulness.* In essence, a Steward must be a believing one. To operate on a high level of Stewardship, you must believe in the King and His Kingdom systems. Faith takes place where the will of God

NOTES

NOTES

is known. What is the will of God for us in this dispensation?

The will of God can only be accomplished by faith, for he that comes to God must believe that He is, that He truly exists first, then he must believe God is a rewarder of those who seek Him.

The Will of God:

- To love God
- To serve God
- To worship God
- To serve our fellow man
- To walk in the priority of God's purpose and plan
- To restore what was lost
- To rebuild what was torn down
- To reconcile humanity back to God

SECTION SIX - THE FIRST STEWARD: ADAM

What book of the Bible reveals the creative order of God?

- We see in _____, chapter two, the order of the creative process. Since all natural things flow from a _____ source, God finishes His work _____ first, then manifests that work in a _____ reality.

- This is why He knows the _____ from the _____.

- This is why the Scripture says that all things were _____ from the _____ of the _____.

- This is why we can have this _____ in His _____ for our lives. Everything about us has been _____ before our parents gave birth to us. Your life is _____ together with Christ in God. God does all things well so there is no need to worry about _____, _____, or _____.

Discuss the first habitat of man:

What is the revelation of God's support?

- The Garden of Eden is known as the region of Adam's ____.

- When we look at the nature of God, He never creates without _____ and He never creates without _____.

- Verse eight says, *He planted a garden eastward in Eden; and there put the man who he had formed.* He created a safe haven to _____ the man's supportive environment that sustains him.

- The Father creates every tree that is pleasant to the sight and good for food. Then He creates the Tree of Life in the midst of the Garden and the Tree of Knowledge of Good and Evil; all in the Garden where man lived.

NOTES

Then God gives Adam the _____ of _____.

- When we look at Genesis, we see the law of _____ mention. The law of first mention carries with it God's _____ intent for that spoken decree.

- God always _____ and _____ what He creates.

- Because provision, protection, and peace are part of ____ plan, I can make my _____ as a Kingdom Steward my priority.

Did Adam have responsibilities in the Garden?

- We see the first mention of the _____ of man in the Garden.

- The Garden had everything he needed, but he was given the responsibility of _____.

- Adam, you are to dress the Garden.

- *Dress it* means to _____, to serve, to till, and to labor over.

- The King James Version defines it this way: to set at work, be wrought, and worshipper.

What does it mean to keep the Garden?

- Definition means to hedge about guard; generally, to protect, attend to. King James defines it like this: be circumspect, take heed, keep, mark, look narrowly, observe, preserve regard, reserve, save self, sure, wait for, watchman.

The more we define, the clearer our purpose becomes.

a) This is quite a definition of man's function: to observe, preserve, regard, reserve, and to be a watchman.

b) The _____ is a primary function of the man. It is defined like this: to lean forward, to peer into the distance, to observe, and to await.

c) To oversee and _____ everything entrusted to his care.

Let's go through these definitions, being they are the attributes of a Steward:

- A Steward must be _____ and wise. The word *circumspect* gives us the other side of being a Steward.

- The word _____ means: to be prudent, careful, judicial, and focused, along with other words that give us the term balanced.

- In order to be _____, a man must be a student and a teacher.

- You must never get to the place where you think of yourself as _____, all knowing, having all wisdom, in need of no one or nothing to assist you. Even after God's creation of Adam, He looked at His work and said, "It is not good that man should be alone; I will make a helpmate just for him."

- If you are the _____ one in your group, you have _____ yourself to only what you know and from being challenged, stretched, and increased in your soul. Third John says, *You prosper and increase to the level that your soul prospers.*

What is the answer to continued growth?

- *You must have a _____, someone you look up to* and get wisdom and instruction from.

- *You must also have a Main _____ Man, a friend that* you walk with in life, another man who has the same experiences and responsibilities you have; Bible says, a brother whom you can depend upon for sharpening. Iron sharpens Iron.

- *You must have a _____, someone who you are* reaching out to as a teacher and a guide. When you are sowing into someone else's life, you are completing the cycle of student/teacher that keeps you balanced.

- This kind of flow keeps _____ coming in and going out. The more you teach what you know the greater your capacity becomes for learning.

NOTES

NOTES

_____
_____
_____
_____
_____
_____
_____
_____
_____
_____
_____
_____
_____
_____
_____
_____
_____
_____
_____
_____
_____
_____
_____
_____
_____
_____
_____
_____

What can derail me as a Steward?

- One of the Achilles heels for men is the misunderstanding of _____ and _____.

- Humility is not a sign of weakness, but a sign of _____. You have the right _____ of yourself and pride cannot override possible _____. Submission is not giving away your _____, but the creation of a _____ to greater power. Submission and humility are the keys to _____ transfer. You can only acquire what you are _____ to _____ to as a covering.

- The difference between a _____ and a _____ needs to be explained.

- A _____ is there to keep things in, to contain and not allow access out.

- A _____ is there to draw out of you what is in you. A covering creates an environment of learning, growing, and maturing as well as activation and manifestation of gifts and talents.

How important is submission in a Steward's life?

- Remember, MOVE Men, one of your most valuable assets for balance is _____. When you have no _____ upstream, you are fishing from a dead sea.

- The lake must have a source from _____ as well as an outlet _____, without these no new things can get in and no old things can get out.

- This is an indication of _____, which produces _____ in a man's life. Growth and change is a product of new knowledge.

- When we are not _____, we are not growing.

- The Bible says, _My people perish for a lack of _____ or because they have rejected knowledge._

What are the limitations on my growth?

- We can only _____to the level of what we _____.

- Jesus said, "And you shall know the truth and the truth you know shall set you free."

- So it is not just knowing a lot of things, but understanding the knowledge you have and _____ it.

- He also said, *"Continue in my word and you shall be my disciples indeed."* The focus word being _____, we must have a hunger and thirst to learn. There is a biblical promise that goes along with a passion to learn. He that hungers and thirsts for _____ shall be filled.

- If the passion for learning is _____ we begin to lose ground. Instead of being _____, we become _____ going backwards.

- We were made to be spiritually_____, ever learning, living, and loving to maintain soundness of mind and preservation of soul.

- We were created to be_____, providers, and _____. That is the reason we have the stronger bodies and we were given a system of focus that brings _____and _____to the family. Our families can trust us to keep them safe; they can rely upon us to provide for their needs on a regular basis, and be their _____ to stand on throughout life.

NOTES

THE FAITH OF THE STEWARD

The Faithful Steward

With any Kingdom mandate comes a requirement of faith. You must believe in the One who called you. You must believe in the proficiency of the gifts, talents, and skills sets you possess to manifests God's purposes. Remember, all good and perfect gifts come down from the Father of lights with whom is no variableness of turning. That means, He does not change His mind about His purposes for your life and will not take away the endowment because of irresponsibility. Gifts and callings are without repentance. Gifts and callings are the plan of God for an individual to experience and live out during his life in the earth. Your unbelief or mistrust or disobedience does not alter the divine blueprints for your life. On the day you are required to give an account for your Stewardship, you will be judged according to His will and not your desire. This is why it is imperative that men believe in God and connect with Him, believe in their call and pursue it passionately and be confident that He who started a good work in them will complete that work before their time is up on earth.

Whenever I am in need of revelation or interpretation of mysteries, I either go to Genesis or to Jesus to find the truth of the matter. Jesus revealed many secrets about Kingdom success and how to live out a successful Kingdom life. His dialogue with Peter just before the crucifixion was enlightening.

NOTES

NOTES

The conversation takes place in **Luke 22:31** - *Then the Lord said, "Simon, Simon, listen! Satan has demanded to have you apostles for himself. He wants to separate you from me as a farmer separates wheat from husks. 32 But I have prayed for you, Simon, that your faith will not fail. So when you recover, strengthen the other disciples."*

Jesus said that Satan had desired and gained permission to test Peter to see if his connection to Christ was authentic and genuine. He assured him the trial was going to come, but that he had prayed for his faith, that his faith was strong enough to recover him from the snare of the devil. The take-away lesson for this story is that the only failure a believer will experience is a faith-failure.

The same truths are located in the book of Genesis known as the Book of Beginnings. Whatever you want to know about the established order, you can find here in this first book of the Bible or in the Gospels of Jesus Christ.

A good Steward must be a man of faith.

Genesis 3:8 - *And they heard the voice of the Lord God walking in the garden in the cool of the day; and Adam and his wife hid themselves from the presence of the Lord God amongst the trees of the garden. 9 And the Lord God called unto Adam, and said unto him, where art thou? 10 And he said I head thy voice in the garden and I was afraid because I was naked and I hid myself. 11 And he sad who told thee that thou wast naked? Hast thou eaten of the tree, whereof I commanded thee that thou shouldest not eat? 12 And the man said, the woman whom thou gavest to be with me, she gave me of the tree, and I did eat. 13 And the Lord God said unto the woman, what is this that thou hast done?* **And the woman said the serpent beguiled me and I did eat.** *14 And the lord God said unto the serpent because thou hast done this thou art cursed above all cattle and above every beast of the field; upon thy belly shalt thou go and dust shalt thou eat all the days of thy life. 15 And I will put enmity between thee and the woman, and between thy seed and her seed; it shall bruise thy head, and thou shalt bruise his heel. 16 Unto the woman he said I will greatly multiply thy sorrow and thy conception in sorrow thou shalt bring forth children; and thy desire shall be to thy husband and he shall rule over thee.* <u>*17 And unto Adam he said because thou hast hearkened unto the voice of they wife, and hast eaten o the tree, of which I commanded*</u>

thee, saying, thou shalt not eat of it; cursed is the ground for thy sake; in sorrow shalt thou eat of it all the days of thy life; 18 Thorns also and thistles shall it bring firth to thee; and thou shalt eat the herb of the field; 19 IN the sweat of thy face shalt thou eat bread, till thou return unto the ground; for out of it wast thou taken; for dust thou art, and unto dust shalt thou return. 20 And Adam called his wife name Eve; because she was the mother of all living. 21 Unto Adam also and to his wife did the Lord God make coats of skins and clothed them.

22 And the Lord 'god said behold the man is become as one of us, to know good and evil and now lest he put forth his hand, and take also of the tree of life, and eat, and live forever: 23 Therefore the Lord God sent him forth from the garden of Eden, to till the ground from whence he was taken. 24 So he drove out the man; and he placed at the east of the Garden of Eden Cherubim's and a flaming sword, which turned every way to keep the way of the tree of life. (KJV)

God made Adam the pattern.

He walked with Adam personally, instructing, training, coaching, and mentoring him to rule over the works of his hands. God's hands on coaching with Adam was intentional so that the pattern for the human race could be set. The interruption of this mentoring process could easily be traced to two simple things.

Why did the fall take place?

It simply comes down to a lack of faith and the misunderstanding of purpose.

- For Eve – misunderstanding of purpose
- For Adam – lack of faith

If you believe Him, you will trust Him, and then you will obey Him.

Belief, trust, and *obedience* are the foundation stones of Faith. With these best practices, one will be able to overcome the fiery darts and snares of the wicked one. Faith was given as a weapon to overcome adversarial challenges as we pursue our purpose in God.

A Steward must fight a disconnect; he must resist derailing ambitions; he must be determined to follow righteousness.

NOTES

NOTES

a) You have to fight – the enemy's offer of doubt and skepticism.

b) You have to resist – the enemy's offer of options and other opinions.

c) You have to make righteous choices – God will not support unrighteousness.

You can only be used to the level of your capacity to control your flesh, resist the devil, and make righteous choices.

REVIEW AND DISCUSSION FOR SECTION SEVEN

THE FAITH OF THE STEWARD

If I am a Steward, why do I need faith?

- With any Kingdom mandate comes a requirement of faith, because your *human* _____is involved. God created you a free moral agent and will not violate your _____l in any way.

- You must _____in the One who called you.

- You must believe in the _____of the gifts, talents, and skills sets you possess to manifest God's purposes. Remember, all good and perfect gifts come down from the Father of lights with whom there is no variableness of turning. That means, He does not change His mind about His _____ for your life and will not take away the _____because of irresponsibility.

- Gifts and callings are without_____.

- Gifts and callings are the plan of God for an individual to _____and live out during his life in the earth.

- Your unbelief or mistrust or disobedience does not alter the divine _____for your life. On the day you are required to give an _____for your Stewardship, you will be judged according to His _____and not your_____. This is why it is imperative that men believe in God and _____ with Him, believe in their call and pursue it passionately and be confident that He who started a good work in them will _____that work before their time is up on earth.

SECTION EIGHT

WALKING WITH GOD

Because of Adam's sin, every man conceived by the seed of man is born with a sin nature; therefore, it is required of every man to seek after God for his personal salvation. Now every man born into the world must seek after the one true and living God. It will not be difficult, because it is the will of God for all men to be saved. When you look for Him, you set in motion the intersection of your connection, because He is looking to walk with you.

James 4:8 - *Draw nigh to God, and he will draw nigh to you. Cleanse your hands, ye sinners; and purify your hearts, ye double minded. 9 Be afflicted, and mourn, and weep: let your laughter be turned to mourning, and your joy to heaviness. 10 Humble yourselves in the sight of the Lord, and he shall lift you up.* (KJV)

Pursuing God should be our top priority.

Hebrews 11:6 - *But without faith it is impossible to please him: for he that cometh to must believe that he is, and that he is a rewarder of them that diligently seek him.* (KJV)

God is looking for His creation to believe Him, to connect with Him, and to walk with Him.

MOVE Men, look at the Patriarchs how they pursued God, how they chased God, and how they believed God. Now it is your turn, your dispensation to chase after the One who created you. In every dispensation, God looks for men who will become radical partners with Him.

God looks for men to walk with Him because He has a plan for each man.

Enoch walked with God.

Genesis 5:21 - *And Enoch lived sixty and five years, and begat Methuselah: 22 and* **_Enoch walked with God_** *after he begat Methuselah three hundred years, and begat sons and daughters: 23 And all the days of Enoch where three hundred sixty and five years: 24* **And Enoch walked with God:** *and he was not; for God took him.*

Noah walked with God.

Genesis 6:9 - *These are the generations of Noah: Noah was a just man and perfect in his generations,* **and Noah walked with God.**

Abraham walked with God.

Genesis 17:1 - *And when Abram was ninety years old and nine, the Lord appeared to Abram, and said unto him,* **I am the almighty God; walk before me,** *and be thou perfect. 2 And I will make my covenant between me and thee, and will multiply thee exceedingly. 3 And Abram fell on his face: and God talked with him, saying.*

What does it take for a man to walk with God?

Hebrews 11:6 - *But without faith it is impossible to please him: for he that cometh to God must believe that he is, and that he is a rewarder of them that diligently seek him.*

When we look carefully at this passage, we see the attributes necessary to walk with God. Let's put them in a list form.

- Must be willing to please God

- Must be willing to come to God

- Must be willing to believe He exists and He alone is God

- Must be willing to believe that He rewards faith in Him

REVIEW AND DISCUSSION FOR SECTION EIGHT

WALKING WITH GOD

Can't I walk with God on the basis of my goodness?

- No, based on the _____ of our father Adam, we are all born into sin.

- Now every man born into the world must _____ after the one true and living God. It will not be difficult, because it is the will of God for all men to be saved.

- When you look for Him you set in _____ the intersection of your connection, because He is looking to walk with you.

What is God looking for?

- God is looking for His creation to _____ Him, to connect with Him, and to _____ with Him.

- MOVE Men, look at the Patriarchs how they pursued God, how they chased God, and how they believed God. Now it is your turn, your _____ to chase after the One who created you.

- In every dispensation, God looks for men who will become radical _____ with Him.

What does it take to walk with God?

- Must be willing to _____ God

- Must be willing to _____ to God

- Must be willing to believe He _____ and He alone is God

- Must be willing to believe that He _____ faith in Him

SECTION NINE

JUSTIFIED BY GOD

It is required that all stewards must first be found faithful. Being faithful as a steward requires living a life of faith. You cannot be faithful without faith; it is your faith that is the justifier. If you believe Him then you are justified by Him.

Hebrews 10:38 - *Now the just shall live by faith; but if any man draw back my soul shall have no pleasure in him. 39 But we are not of them who draw back unto perdition; but of them that believe to the saving of the soul.*

The Scriptures are clear; look at the list:

1. A just Steward lives by faith

2. A just Steward pleases God with his faith

3. A just Steward believes until change takes place

You are justified by faith. That means, you are justified by God for believing in God. Jesus said, "You cannot say you believe me and do not the things that I say." So there is a test you can take to determine your belief. The test of believing is your obedient compliance to God. Every man must ask himself this question: Do I obey God?

It is not what you have on your résumé that makes you the accumulation of past efforts, it is not your wishful positive thinking for the future, but it is your right-now commitment to righteousness. Can you obey God when the instructions make you look inferior to your friends or foolish to your family or even unreasonable to yourself? The question again, MOVE Men, is this: Do I Obey God?

To be a good Steward, you must Believe, Trust, and Obey.

Noah believed God.

Hebrews 11:7 - By faith Noah *being warned of God of things not seen as yet, moved with fear, prepared an ark to the saving of his house; by which he condemned the world, and became heir of the righteousness, which is by faith.*

- Noah believed God and built an ark, though it had never rained or flooded.

- He was willing to look silly in the sight of men.

- He was willing to believe for long extended periods of time.

Abraham believed God.

Hebrews 11:8 - By faith Abraham, *when he was called to go out into a place, which he should after receive for an inheritance, obeyed; and he went out, not knowing whither he went.*

- You must be willing to please God by following God.

- Your obedience must be geological – go to and stay at the place God sends you.

- Your obedience must exceed the borders of your soul.

- Your trust must be of such that you can be led into uncharted territory.

Enoch believed God.

Hebrews 11: 5 - By faith Enoch *was translated that he should not see death; and was not found, because God had translated him: for before his translation he had this testimony, that he pleased God.*

- Enoch was not, because he pleased God.

- Enoch had a testimony, which means that he experienced things that tested his belief and trust in God.

REVIEW AND DISCUSSION FOR SECTION NINE

JUSTIFIED BY GOD

Is faithfulness necessary to function as a Steward?

- It is _____ that all Stewards must first be found faithful.

- Being _____ as a Steward requires living a life of faith.

- You cannot be _____ without faith in; it is your faith that is the _____.

- If you _____ Him then you are _____ by Him.

- You will not _____ what you do not believe.

Faithfulness is a product of living by faith.

Now the just shall live by faith; but if any man draws back, my soul shall have no pleasure in him.

The Scriptures are clear; a Steward must live by faith.

- A just Steward lives by _____.

- A just Steward _____ God with his faith.

- A just Steward believes until his faith produces _____.

What is the pillar of my faith?

- You are _____ by faith. That means you are justified by God for believing in God. Jesus said, "You cannot say you believe me and do not the things that I say."

- So there is a test you can take to _____ the barometer of your belief.

- The test of believing is your _____ compliance to God. Every man must ask himself this question: Do I obey God?

- It is not what you have on your _____ that makes you, that is, the accumulation of past efforts, it is not your wishful positive thinking for the future, but it is your right-now _____ to righteousness.

- Can you obey God when the instructions make you look _____ to your friends or _____ to your family or even _____ to yourself?

- The question again, MOVE Men, is this: Do I _____ God?

- To be a good _____ you must believe, trust, and obey.

NOTES

SECTION TEN

GOD IS LOOKING FOR A STEWARD

For God to get His plan accomplished He must seek out a man in the earth to partner with. He is looking for a man to believe Him. He is looking for a man to trust Him. He is looking for a man to obey Him. He is looking for a man to walk with Him. He is looking for a man who will be a wise and faithful Steward.

God always looks for a man to send to accomplish His plan.

1. Adam was created the first man to give birth to the human race.

2. His sin called for another Adam to be sent to redeem back what was lost through his disobedience.

3. God will keep sending men with parts of the plan to execute, but they must be willing to stay with their assignment and not give into options and opinions.

4. There are assignments made for men and certain men for assignments. For example, Moses was chosen to deliver Israel, but God rose up Joshua to finish the work. But the assignment of salvation could not be passed on to another – it could only be given to Jesus.

5. Every man has his assignment; that particular function makes him special and unique to the plan of God.

God is always looking for a man who will qualify as a good steward of the manifold grace that is on his life to accept and carry out the call, the commission, and the trust.

John 1:6 - *<u>There was a man sent from God, whose name was John</u>. 7 The same came for a witness, to bear witness of the Light, that all men through him might believe. 8 He was not that Light, but was sent to bear witness of that Light. 9 That was the true light, which lighteth every man that cometh into the world.*

God sent John into the earth with a specific assignment.

- He was not the Christ, but the forerunner to the Christ.

- He was not the light, but was to bear witness of the light.

- So his job was to be His witness and a voice for somebody coming later – this is the work of a steward. Can you be a voice to support the main character? When you are faithful to your assignment you become a critical component to the success of God's plan.

- When Jesus came, John's disciples did not understand his assignment and got jealous. When you know your assignment, you will not be threatened by someone else's.

John corrects the thinking of his disciples regarding Stewardship.

John 3:27 - *John answered and said, a man can receive nothing, except it be given him from heaven.*

- God only gives you the grace for your assignment.

- You will only have satisfaction when you are in your assignment and embrace it fully.

- A man on the move for God embraces his assignment.

- MOVE Men on the move resist options and opinions and embrace their God-given assignment.

NOTES

REVIEW AND DISCUSSION FOR SECTION TEN

GOD IS LOOKING FOR A STEWARD

Does God really need me in His plan?

- For God to get His plan accomplished, He must seek out a man in the earth to _____ with.

- He is looking for a man to _____ Him.

- He is looking for a man to _____ Him.

- He is looking for a man to _____ Him.

- He is looking for a man to _____ with Him.

- He is looking for a man who will be a wise and faithful_____.

God always looks for a man to send to accomplish His plan.

- Adam was created the _____man to give birth to the human race.

- His sin called for _____Adam to be sent to redeem back what was lost.

- God will keep sending _____with parts of the plan to execute, but they must be willing to stay with their _____and not give into options and opinions.

- There are _____made for men and certain men for_____. For example, Moses was chosen to deliver Israel, but God rose up Joshua to finish the work. But the _____of salvation could not be passed on to another – it could only be given to Jesus.

God is always looking for a man who will qualify as a good Steward of the manifold grace that is on his life to accept and carry out the call, the commission, and the trust.

Who gives the Steward his assignment?

- John answered and said, *"A man can receive nothing, except it be given him from_____."*

- God only gives you the _____ for your assignment.

- A man on the move for God _____ his assignment.

- MOVE Men on the move _____options and opinions and embrace their God-given assignment.

- You will only have _____ when you are in your assignment and embrace it fully.

SECTION ELEVEN

HINDRANCES TO THE STEWARD

John quickly extinguished his disciples' pride.

John 3:26 - *And they came unto John, and said unto him, Rabbi, he that was with thee beyond Jordan, to whom thou barest witness, behold, the same baptizeth, and all men come to him. 27 John answered and said, a man can receive nothing, except it be given him from heaven. 28 Ye yourselves bear me witness, that I said, I am not the Christ, but that I am sent before him. (KJV)*

Sometimes the problem comes – when negative motivators influence us in a wrong way.

The Steward must control his emotions:

- **ego** – self-importance / thinking more highly than you should

- **pride** – arrogance or majesty / haughtiness, highness, pride, swelling

- **arrogance** – conceit, pride, self-importance, egotism / making claims or pretentions to superior importance or rights: overbearingly assuming: insolently proud

Unbridled ambition – unrestrained or uncontrolled desires, motivations, or zeal

- Beyond your channel to receive – doors of favor are closed

- Beyond your capacity to create – skill, talent, anointing

- Beyond your purpose to produce – assignment

- Beyond your grace capacity – you want it, but God did not give that grace to you

All of these are signs to the Steward of potential derailment.

- God gives us what we need to succeed in the assignment He gives us.

Romans 12:3 - *For I say though the grace given unto me to every man that is among you not to think of himself more highly than he ought to think; but to think soberly according as God hath dealt to every man the measure of Faith.*

- God gives each man the measure of faith according to the grace on him for his assignment.

- When you operate outside your grace, productivity does not take place.

Satanic Strategies to Ensnare the Steward

- The lust of the flesh – you will be like God

- The lust of the eyes – saw it was good for food

- The pride of life – desired to make one wise

Make sure what you are ascribing to do has come from God and not from friends, family, or ego.

REVIEW AND DISCUSSION SECTION ELEVEN

HINDRANCES TO THE STEWARD

Sometimes the problem comes – when _____ motivators _____ us in a wrong way.

What emotions must the Steward control?

- _____ – self-importance / thinking more highly than you should

- _____ – arrogance or majesty / haughtiness, highness, pride, swelling

- _____ – conceit, pride, self-importance, egotism / making claims or pretentions to superior importance or rights: overbearingly assuming: insolently proud

What is unbridled ambition?

Unbridled ambition – unrestrained or uncontrolled desires, motivations, or zeal

- Beyond your channel to _____ – doors of favor are closed

- Beyond your capacity to _____ – skill, talent, anointing

- Beyond your purpose to _____ – assignment

- Beyond your grace _____ – you want it, but God did not give that grace to you

- All of these are _____ to the Steward of potential derailment

What are some Satanic Strategies to Ensnare the Steward?

- The lust of the _____ – you will be like God

- The lust of the _____ – saw it was good for food

- The pride of _____ – desired to make one wise

Make sure what you are ascribing to do has come from God and not from friends, family, or ego.

- God gives us what we need to _____in the assignment He gives us.

- God gives each man the _____of faith according to the grace on him for his assignment.

- When you operate _____your grace, productivity does not take place.

SECTION TWELVE

ANOINTED TO BE YOU

John was the miracle child of Zachariah and Elisabeth who was barren in her young age. But the angel visited them and said their prayer was heard and she would bare a special child.

John was totally focused on his Stewardship.

- He totally embraced who he was.

- He totally embraced what he was sent to do.

- He totally knew who he was not.

John 1:22 - *Then they said to him, "Who are you, that we may give an answer to those who sent us? What do you say about yourself?" 23 He said: "I am 'The voice of one crying in the wilderness: 'Make straight the way of the Lord,"' as the prophet Isaiah said." 24 Now those who were sent were from the Pharisees. 25 And they asked him, saying, "Why then do you baptize if you are not the Christ, nor Elijah, nor the Prophet?" 26 John answered them, saying, "I baptize with water, but there stands One among you whom you do not know. 27 It is He who, coming after me, is preferred before me, whose sandal strap I am not worthy to loose." 28 These things were done in Bethabara beyond the Jordan, where John was baptizing.* (NKJV)

Then John is born – but the Scripture says he was sent from God.

- He was sent to make straight the way of the Lord.

- He was sent to be a voice crying in the wilderness.

- He was sent as a forerunner to Christ.

God sent you here – you must discover why you are here.

- If you don't know, ask Him.

- James said, *"If you lack wisdom ask God who gives liberally to all who ask."*

- Once you pray, be ready to obey.

- Every time I asked God about my assignment He gave.

I anoint myself to walk with God every day.

- To walk in study with the Holy Spirit

- To walk in prayer

- To walk in holiness

- To walk in deliverance

- To walk in discipline

- To walk in divine health

- To walk in divine wealth

- To walk as a devoted leader

- To walk as a diligent entrepreneur

- To walk dedicated to my calling as an Apostle

Is there an option?

- Because of *free will* you can make whatever choice you want to make.

- Adam failed because he used *free will* to choose something else.

- Adam took the option, but he was not happy or fulfilled.

But let's run some references in the Bible to see if faith is a divine requirement.

Salvation requires faith!

Romans 10:8 - *But what saith it? The word is nigh thee, even I nth youth and in thy heart that is the word of faith which we*

NOTES

*preach; 9 That if thou shalt confess with thy mouth the Lord Jesus, and shalt believe in thine heart that God hath raised him from the dead, thou shalt be saved. 10 For **with the heart** man believeth unto righteousness; and **with the mouth** confession is made unto salvation.*

To be a son of God requires faith!

Galatians 3:26 - *For ye are all the children of God by faith in Christ Jesus.*

To see the power of God requires faith!

Romans 1:16 - *For I am not ashamed of the gospel of Christ; for it is the power of God unto salvation to everyone that believeth; to the Jew first, and also to the Greek. 17 For therein is the righteousness of God revealed from faith to faith; as it is written the just shall live by faith.* (KJV)

The walk of faith includes:

- The practice of faith – use faith daily

- Use faith for family protection and provision

- Use faith for ultimate fitness – your health and emotional and mental welfare

- Use faith for accessing your future - what God has for you as you grow in God. At 17, Joseph was not ready; he grew in stature for 13 or so years before he was ready for his assignment.

- Use faith for increased finances. You are at the level of your belief. Increase your faith.

All Kingdom work requires faith!

James 2:18 - *Yea, a man may say, thou hast faith, and I have works: shew me thy faith without thy works, and I will shew thee my faith by my works. 19 Thou believest that there is one God; thou doest well: the devils also believe, and tremble. 20 But wilt thou know, O vain man, that faith without works is dead?* (KJV)

Every man has starting faith!

Romans 12:3 - *For I say, through the grace given unto me, to every man that is among you, not to think of himself more highly than he* *ought to think; but to think soberly, according as God hath dealt to every man the measure of faith.* (KJV)

- Every man has been given the measure of faith.

- When you come into the Kingdom of God, you are given a deposit of faith.

- So every man is given a starting point but not an ending point.

- You can go as high as you allow yourself to go.

In order to grow in anything, there must be friction or resistance.

- If a person is weak, the only way to get strong is to exercise the weak muscle.

- Unless we function in faith, we lose the capacity to work continually.

All Stewards are required to walk by faith, not by sight.

2 Corinthians 5:6 - *Therefore we are always confident, knowing that, whilst we are at home in the body, we are absent from the Lord: 7 For we walk by faith, not by sight.*

We live by what we believe, not by what we can see.

If you live only by what you can see, you will limit yourself to what is possible by faith.

Do not allow what you see before you to be your finality; only God sets the perimeter of a man's life.

He created you to live an abundant life.

He created you to manage the works of His hands.

He created you to overcome the world system.

He created you to have dominion.

He created you to be His faithful Steward.

NOTES

REVIEW AND DISCUSSION FOR SECTION TWELVE

ANOINTED TO BE YOU

Then John is born – but the Scripture says he was sent from God.

He was sent to make_____ the way of the Lord.

He was sent to be a _____crying in the wilderness.

He was sent as a _____to Christ.

John was totally focused on his Stewardship.

He totally embraced who he_____.

He totally embraced what he was sent to_____.

He totally knew who he was_____.

God sent you here – you must discover why you are here.

- Is there an_____?

- Because of *free will,* you can make whatever _____ you want to make.

- Adam failed because he used *free will* to _____ something else.

- Adam took the _____but he was not happy or fulfilled.

- If you don't know, _____ Him.

- James said – if you lack_____, ask God who gives liberally to all who ask.

- Once you pray, be ready to_____.

- Every time I asked God about my_____, He gave instructions.

- God wants you to _____as a Steward; your success glorifies Him.

I believe in my assignment, so I anoint myself every day for it.

I embrace it with all my heart, mind, and soul.

My main priority is to please God with my life.

I want to serve God by serving His purposes, which is my destiny.

A Declaration of Faith as a Kingdom Steward

I anoint myself to walk with God every day:

- To walk in study with the Holy Spirit
- To walk in prayer
- To walk in holiness
- To walk in deliverance
- To walk in discipline
- To walk in divine health
- To walk in divine wealth
- To walk as a devoted leader
- To walk as a diligent entrepreneur
- To walk dedicated to my calling as an Apostle

On a daily basis, what should I use my faith on?

The walk of faith includes:

- The practice of faith – you use faith daily for personal_____.
- Use faith for your _____ protection and provision and peace.
- Use faith for ultimate _____ – your health and emotional mental welfare.
- Use faith for accessing your _____ – what God has for you as you grow in God.
- Use faith for increased _____. You are at the level of your belief. Increase your faith, and increase will come to your finances.

NOTES

NOTES

_____

Walk by faith, not by sight.

- Every man has been given the _____of faith.

- When you come into the Kingdom of God, you are given a deposit of_____.

- So every man is given a _____point, but not an ending point.

- You can go as high as you _____yourself to go.

In order to grow in anything, there must be friction or resistance.

- If a person is weak, the only way to get strong is to _____the weak muscle.

- Unless we function in faith, we lose the capacity to work_____.

- Build your f_____ muscle every day.

We live by what we believe not by what we can see.

- If you live only by what you can see, you will _____yourself to what is possible by faith.

- Do not allow what you see before you to be your_____; only God sets the perimeter of a man's life.

- He created you to live an _____life.

- He created you to _____the works of His hands.

- He created you to _____the world system.

- He created you to have _____.

- He created you to be His _____ and _____ Steward.

SECTION THIRTEEN

LIFE AS A STEWARD

Stewardship as a Single Man:

1 Thessalonians 4:1 - *One final word, friends. We ask you — urge is more like it — that you keep on doing what we told you to do to please God, not in a dogged religious plod, but in a living, spirited dance. 2 You know the guidelines we laid out for you from the Master Jesus. 3 God wants you to live a pure life. Keep yourselves from sexual promiscuity. 4 Learn to appreciate and give dignity to your body, 5 not abusing it, as is so common among those who know nothing of God. 6 Don't run roughshod over the concerns of your brothers and sisters. Their concerns are God's concerns, and he will take care of them. We've warned you about this before. 7 God hasn't invited us into a disorderly, unkempt life but into something holy and beautiful — as beautiful on the inside as the outside. 8 If you disregard this advice, you're not offending your neighbors; you're rejecting God, who is making you a gift of his Holy Spirit. 9 Regarding life together and getting along with each other, you don't need me to tell you what to do. You're God-taught in these matters. Just love one another! 10 You're already good at it; your friends all over the province of Macedonia are the evidence. Keep it up; get better and better at it. 11 Stay calm; mind your own business; do your own job. You've heard all this from us before, but a reminder never hurts. 12 We want you living in a way that will command the respect of outsiders, not lying around sponging off your friends.* (MSG)

Paul's exhortation included a checklist for all men:

- Walking with God to please Him.

- Sanctification is the will of God so that we abstain from fornication.

- Know how to possess your body in sanctification and honor.

- Do not defraud your brothers in any matter – the Lord will avenge.

- God has called us to holiness not uncleanness.

- Increase more and more in love for others.

- Study to be quiet.

- Do your own business.

- Work with your own hands.

- Do this so you can be honest and that you lack nothing.

How do we possess our vessels in sanctification and honor?

Self-Government is the highest form of government there is; a man must be able to control himself, manage his appetites, dominate his passions, make righteous choices, yield to authority, and walk with God.

Vision Progressive – do something with your life; make an impact upon your generation by obeying the call of God on your life.

It is imperative that every man has a vision for his life. Without a vision, he will fall prey to perilous predicaments. Why?

- Because of lack of focus to pay attention to purpose.

- Because of lack of fortitude to follow through and finish.

- Because of lack of faith to acquire the supernatural power to produce fruit.

NOTES

NOTES

Every man must manage himself!

Manage your mind

- ✓ School – educate yourself
- ✓ Social – interact with others
- ✓ Society – be a good citizen

Manage your body

- ✓ Healthy fitness plan
- ✓ Nutrition plan – right diet
- ✓ Medical plan – know your body

Manage your spirit

- ✓ Spiritual growth – word
- ✓ Spiritual service – post
- ✓ Spiritual sowing – giving

When a single man is a good Steward of his life, he has become capable of taking on a wife, if he so chooses.

When a man masters himself, his faithfulness has qualified him for higher-level Stewardship, which is the care of others.

Stewardship as a Married Man

1 Peter 3:7 - *In the same way you married men should live considerately with your wives, with an intelligent recognition of the marriage relationship, honoring the woman as physically the weaker, but realizing that you are joint heirs of the grace, Gods unmerited favor of life, in order that your prayers may not be hindered and cut off. Otherwise you cannot pray effectively.*

The exhortation included these mandates:

Live considerately – be thoughtful

- To think of or consider in a particular way; to look at attentively; to observe closely.
- To be concerned.
- To show regard for her feelings and needs.

- Being thoughtful is something every husband must master if he is to enjoy being married. Being attentive, having regard for her feelings, and meeting her needs come with high dividends.

Live in intelligent recognition of the marriage relationship

- According to knowledge – knowing the science, act, study her to know how she works; to understand her, know how she feels.

Live honoring the woman as physically weaker

- Means less in physical strength, which gives the husband the responsibility of taking away things that are overwhelming.

- The word *honor* means – to place a value on, to make valuable; to esteem, which is of the highest degree; dignity itself.

Live realizing God made both of you joint heirs of the grace

- The value we put on our wives and the dignity we show them are the qualifying factors for the flow of grace into the relationship. The grace we participate in together produces benefit, favor, gift, grace, joy, liberality, and pleasure.

Living opposite to these truths affects your prayer life.

- **First Phase is a Hindered Prayer Life** – impede, detain; delayed answers to your prayer.

- **Second Phase is a Cut-Off Prayer Life** – cuts into; your bad behavior towards your wife cuts into your relationship with God and a breach occurs. You need to get this right before you enter into the third stage. This stage is frustrating and tedious.

- **Third Phase is an Ineffective Prayer Life** – not working, none fruitful; you are now in a religious zone and your relationship with God is out of tradition. Get right with your wife and rescue yourself from this stage; you could spend years being unproductive.

NOTES

Additional practices for married life:

Add to self-government ministry to a spouse.

- Have a vision plan for your life – spiritual and natural.

- Embrace the responsibility of covenant – choose wisely, treat kindly.

- Live under the conviction of spousal ministry – you are responsible to minister to her; end results are the fruits of happiness.

- Be your spouse's primary intercessor.

- Practice the principle of agreement.

- Manage your money well – never be caught unprepared; have reserves; always think about her future; get an insurance policy to take care of her when you can't.

Stewardship as a Father

Ephesians 6:4 - *And, ye fathers, provoke not your children to wrath: but bring them up in the nurture and admonition of the Lord.* **(KJV)**

The exhortation is simple:

Fathers, Do not provoke children to wrath.

- Do not irritate them.

- Do not provoke them to anger.

- Do not exasperate them to resentment.

Bring them up in the nurture and admonition of the Lord.

➢ You are responsible for the seed you birth.

➢ You must make a father's deposit into their lives.

➢ You rear them up tenderly in training – teach and inform.

➢ You rear them up tender in discipline – to correct for character modification.

➢ You rear them up tender in counsel – to give advice and guidance and recommendations.

➢ You rear them in the admonition of the Lord – mild, kind, yet earnest reproof; cautionary advice or warning. When you are admonishing a child you are giving them counsel against something that should be avoided because it is dangerous. Something that will take them off the course of Christian ethics.

A Father's Good Practices:

- Be an example, not a dictator

- Be a protector

- Be a provider

- Be a teacher and coach

- Be a father (a caring one)

- Be gentle

- Be kind

- Be an encourager

- Be a spiritual guide

Stewardship to Parents

Ephesians 6:1 - *Children, obey your parents in the Lord: for this is right. 2 Honor thy father and mother; (which is the first commandment with promise;) 3 That it may be well with thee, and thou mayest live long on the earth.* (KJV)

First Concept – loving my parents

When we are in our parents' house, it is critical to show honor. You are actually setting yourself up for a future harvest on the seeds you have sown into their lives. This particular commandment has a promise that many need to recognize if your life is not going well. Research the seed you left in your parents' home. If you are still having trouble in life after so many years of independence you might want to go back and repent for some things. Living long on the earth comes by good behavior. When you do good to others, good comes back to you.

NOTES

NOTES

Second Concept – leaving my parents

Proverbs 18:22 - *Whosoever findeth a wife findeth a good thing, and obtaineth favor of the Lord.* (KJV)

This new relationship now requires an adjustment in lifestyle. It requires a new set of priorities.

Genesis 2:18 - *And the Lord God said, it is not good that the man should be alone; I will make him an help meet for him. 19 And out of the ground the Lord God formed every beast of the field, and every fowl of the air; and brought them unto Adam to see what he would call them: and whatsoever Adam called every living creature, that was the name thereof. 20 And Adam gave names to all cattle, and to the fowl of the air, and to every beast of the field; but for Adam there was not found a helpmate for him. 21 And the Lord God caused a deep sleep to fall upon Adam and he slept: and he took one of his ribs, and closed up the flesh instead thereof; 22 And the rib, which the Lord God had taken from man, made he a woman, and brought her unto the man. 23 And Adam said, this is now bone of my bones, and flesh of my flesh: she shall be called Woman, because she was taken out of Man. 24 Therefore shall a man leave his father and his mother, and shall cleave unto his wife: and they shall be one flesh.*

25 And they were both naked, the man and his wife, and were not ashamed. (KJV)

The exhortation

When a man finds a wife, the Word says, he finds a good thing and obtains favor from the Lord.

But in order for that favor to flourish, he must leave his parents' house to furnish a house for his wife.

- She now becomes the priority of his life.
- She must have first place with his attention.
- She must have first place with his provision.
- She must have first place with his protection.
- She must have first place with his time.

Third Concept – loving my parents

1 Timothy 5:3 - *Take care of widows who are destitute. 4 If a widow has family members to take care of her, let them learn that religion begins at their own doorstep and that they should pay back with gratitude some of what they have received. This pleases God immensely. 5 You can tell a legitimate widow by the way she has put all her hope in God, praying to him constantly for the needs of others as well as her own. 6 But a widow who exploits people's emotions and pocketbooks — well, there's nothing to her. 7 Tell these things to the people so that they will do the right thing in their extended family. 8 Anyone who neglects to care for family members in need repudiates the faith. That's worse than refusing to believe in the first place.*

1 Timothy 5:16 - *Any Christian woman who has widows in her family is responsible for them. They shouldn't be dumped on the church. The church has its hands full already with widows who need help.* (MES)

The exhortation

> ➤ The Word is very clear that families are responsible for their senior parents when age has overtaken them and assistance is warranted.

> ➤ Paul says to be careful for those who would manipulate and exploit using emotions to tap into their children's pocketbooks.

> ➤ But well-deserving parents should receive care in their old age as reciprocation for all their work in your young age.

> ➤ Of course, every family has unique situations; but keep in mind the exhortation and make your adjustments.

> ➤ A husband and wife must come to an agreement in these matters seeing that it is no added pressure and stress.

> ➤ Whatever is to be done must be agreed upon.

> ➤ If your home is not big enough for your parents, then think about putting them in a care facility and visit them there.

NOTES

NOTES

> If your home is big enough and you can agree then lay down some rules for care and fellowship that will include the whole family.

Fourth and Final Concept – Loving My God

Matthew 22:37 - *Jesus said unto him, Thou shalt love the Lord thy God with all thy heart, and with all thy soul, and with all thy mind. 38 This is the first and great commandment. 39 And the second is like unto it, thou shalt love thy neighbor as thyself. 40 On these two commandments hang all the law and the prophets.* (KJV)

The first and greatest Commandment is to love God with all your heart and soul and mind. Jesus says to connect with God with your entire being. He is to be the centerpiece of your heart; He is to be the object of affection for your soul; He is the central thought that dominates your mind. From this description we are to be consumed with His presence. The way it is described is like an addiction. But this addiction is the cornerstone of life itself. Everything we are, everything we have, all comes from this same source; it all comes from God. Let's look at the beginning of this love relationship in the book of Genesis.

Genesis 2:7 - *And the Lord **God formed man** of the dust of the ground, and **breathed into his nostrils** the breath of life; and man became a living soul. 8 And the Lord **God planted a garden** eastward in Eden; and **there he put the man** whom he had formed. 9 And out of the ground made the Lord God to grow **every tree that is pleasant to the sight, and good for food**; the tree of life also in the midst of the garden, and the tree of knowledge of good and evil. 10 And a river went out of Eden to water the garden; and from thence it was parted, and became into four heads. 11 The name of the first is Pison: that is it which compasseth the whole land of Havilah, where there is gold; 12 And the gold of that land is good: there is bdellium and the onyx stone. 13 And the name of the second river is Gihon: the same is it that compasseth the whole land of Ethiopia. 14 And the name of the third river is Hiddekel: that is it which goeth toward the east of Assyria. And the fourth river is Euphrates. 15 And the Lord God took the man, and put him into the garden of Eden to dress it and to keep it. 16 And the Lord God commanded the man, saying, of every tree of the garden thou mayest freely eat: 17 But of the tree of the knowledge of good and evil, thou shalt not eat of it: for in the day that thou eatest thereof* *thou shalt surely die. 18 And the Lord God said, it is not good that the man should be alone;* **I will make him a help meet for him.** *19 And out of the ground the Lord God formed every beast of the field, and every fowl of the air; and* **brought them unto Adam to see what he would call them***: and whatsoever Adam called every living creature, that was the name thereof. 20 And Adam gave names to all cattle, and to the fowl of the air, and to every beast of the field; but for Adam there was not found an help meet for him. 21 And the Lord God caused a deep sleep to fall upon Adam and he slept: and he took one of his ribs, and closed up the flesh instead thereof; 22 And the rib, which the Lord God had taken from man, made he a woman, and brought her unto the man.*

23 And Adam said, This is now bone of my bones, and flesh of my flesh: she shall be called Woman, because she was taken out of Man.

24 Therefore shall a man leave his father and his mother, and shall cleave unto his wife: and they shall be one flesh. 25 And they were both naked, the man and his wife, and were not ashamed. (KJV)

MOVE Men, it is crucial for every man to have a relationship with God. It is important for each one of us to know the law of connection. Whatever it took to start life is necessary to continue life. Man cannot live his best life apart from the One who created him. It was the Father God who created Adam, fellowshipped daily with him, taught and trained him in his faith. It was He, who provided shelter, support, sustenance, and a spouse for his survival in this strange new world.

Look at the love of God! He made the man, gave him life, made him a home, gave him Stewardship and ruler-ship. Gave him rules for accountability, and did not want him to live life alone, so he made him a helpmate. He made him in His own image and likeness, then gave him dominion over all the earth. He then blessed him and commissioned him to be fruitful, multiply, and replenish the earth and subdue it. What a love story. All He is asking from us is to be good Stewards and function in our commission. Be fruitful, multiply, and replenish all made possible through our connection with Him.

The Steward's Connection

John 15:1 - *I am the Real Vine and my Father is the Farmer. 2 He cuts off every branch of me that doesn't bear grapes. And every*

NOTES

NOTES

branch that is grape-bearing he prunes back so it will bear even more. 3 You are already pruned back by the message I have spoken.

4 "Live in me. Make your home in me just as I do in you. In the same way that a branch can't bear grapes by itself but only by being joined to the vine, you can't bear fruit unless you are joined with me.

5 "I am the Vine; you are the branches. When you're joined with me and I with you, the relation intimate and organic, the harvest is sure to be abundant. Separated, you can't produce a thing. 6 Anyone who separates from me is deadwood, gathered up and thrown on the bonfire. 7 But if you make yourselves at home with me and my words are at home in you, you can be sure that whatever you ask will be listened to and acted upon. 8 This is how my Father shows who he is — when you produce grapes, when you mature as my disciples.

9 "I've loved you the way my Father has loved me. Make yourselves at home in my love. 10 If you keep my commands, you'll remain intimately at home in my love. That's what I've done — kept my

Father's commands and made myself at home in his love. 11 "I've told you these things for a purpose: that my joy might be your joy, and your joy wholly mature. 12 This is my command: Love one another the way I loved you. 13 This is the very best way to love. Put your life on the line for your friends. 14 You are my friends when you do the things I command you. 15 I'm no longer calling you servants because servants don't understand what their master is thinking and planning. No, I've named you friends because I've let you in on everything I've heard from the Father. 16 "You didn't choose me, remember; I chose you, and put you in the world to bear fruit, fruit that won't spoil. As fruit bearers, whatever you ask the Father in relation to me, he gives you. 17 "But remember the root command: Love one another. (MSG)

Just like in Matthew, Jesus repeats it in John. Submerge yourself in God. With this connection that we have in Him, it is impossible not to be fruitful. The key is staying connected. That is what that escapade in the Garden of Eden was all about. Satan was trying to disrupt and disconnect Adam and Eve from their source. The same occurred with Job when Satan accused him of not really loving God with all his heart, but just for what he could get from God. It was all about the relationship, nothing more - nothing less. MOVE Men, the key to our life is our connection with God.

Connection is the key to thriving as a Steward.

- Connection is the key to potential – made in His image and likeness

- Connection is the key to opportunity – given authority to rule

- Connection is the key to productivity – bear fruit

- Connection is the key to creativity – mentored for elevated faith

- Connection is the key to possibility – highest lifestyle possible

- Connection is the key to posterity – power to multiply, make more than one

NOTES

NOTES

REVIEW AND DISCUSSION FOR SECTION THIRTEEN

LIFE AS A STEWARD

Stewardship as a Single Man

Paul's exhortation included a checklist for all men:

- Walking with God to _____ Him

- _____ is the will of God that we abstain from fornication

- Know how to _____ your body in sanctification and honor

- Do not _____ your brothers in any matter – the Lord will avenge

- God has called us to _____ not uncleanness

- Increase more and more in _____ for others

- Study to be _____

- Do your own _____

- Work with your own _____

- Do this so you can be honest and that you lack _____

How do we possess our vessels in sanctification and honor?

_____ – it is the highest form of government there is; a man must be able to control himself, manage his appetites, dominate his passions, make righteous choices, yield to authority, and walk with God.

_____ – do something with your life; make an impact upon your generation by obeying the call of God on your life.

It is imperative that every man has a vision for his life. Without a vision he will fall prey to perilous predicaments. Why?

- Because of lack of focus to pay attention to purpose.

- Because of lack of fortitude to follow through and finish.

- Because of lack of faith to acquire the supernatural power to produce fruit.

Every man must manage himself!

<u>**Manage your mind**</u>

✓ School – educate _____

✓ Social – interact with _____

✓ Society – be a good _____

<u>**Manage your body**</u>

✓ Healthy _____ plan

✓ Nutrition plan – right _____

✓ Medical plan – know your _____

<u>**Manage your spirit**</u>

✓ Spiritual growth – _____

✓ Spiritual service – _____

✓ Spiritual sowing – _____

When a single man is a good _____ of his life, he has become capable of taking on a wife, if he so chooses.

When a man _____ himself, his faithfulness has qualified him for higher-level Stewardship, which is the care of others.

Stewardship as a Married Man

The exhortation included these mandates:

Live considerately – be thoughtful

- To think of or consider in a particular way; to look at_____; to observe closely

- To be _____

NOTES

NOTES

- To show _____ for her feelings and needs

- Being _____ is something every husband must master if he is to enjoy being married. Being attentive, having regard for her feelings and meeting her needs come with high dividends.

Live in intelligent recognition of the marriage relationship.

- According to _____ – knowing the science, act, study her to know how she works; to understand her; know how she feels.

Live honoring the woman as physically weaker.

- Means less in physical _____, which gives the husband the responsibility of taking away things that are overwhelming.

- The word _____r means: to place a value on to make valuable; to esteem, which is of the highest degree; dignity itself.

Live realizing God made both of you joint heirs of the grace.

- The _____ we put on our wives, the _____ we show them is the _____ factor for the flow of grace into the relationship. The grace we participate in together produces benefit, favor, gift, grace, joy, liberality, and pleasure.

Living opposite to these truths affects your prayer life.

- First phase is a _____ Prayer-Life – impede, detain; delayed answers to your prayers.

- Second phase is a _____ Prayer-Life – cuts into; your bad behavior towards your wife cuts into your relationship with God; a breach occurs. You need to get this right before you enter into the third stage. This stage is frustrating and tedious.

- Third phase is an _____ Prayer-Life – not working; none fruitful; you are now in a religious zone and your relationship with God is out of tradition. Get right with your wife and rescue yourself from this stage. You could spend years being unproductive.

Additional practices for married life:

Add to self-government ministry to a spouse

- Have a _____plan for your life – spiritual and natural.

- Embrace the responsibility of _____ – choose wisely, treat kindly.

- Live under the _____of spousal ministry – you are responsible to minister to her; end results are the fruits of happiness.

- Be your spouse's primary_____.

- Practice the principle of_____.

- Manage your _____well – never be caught unprepared, have reserves; always think about her future; get an insurance policy to take care of her when you can't.

Stewardship as a Father

The exhortation is simple:

Fathers, do not provoke children to wrath.

- ❖ Do not _____them.

- ❖ Do not _____them to anger.

- ❖ Do not _____ them to resentment.

Bring them up in the nurture and admonition of the Lord.

- ➤ You are _____for the seed you birth.

- ➤ You must make a father's _____into their lives.

- ➤ You rear them up tenderly in _____ – teach, inform.

- ➤ You rear them up tender in _____ – to correct for character modification.

- ➤ You rear them up tender in _____ – to give advice and guidance and recommendations.

NOTES

NOTES

_____
_____
_____
_____
_____
_____
_____
_____
_____
_____
_____
_____
_____
_____
_____
_____
_____
_____
_____
_____
_____
_____
_____
_____
_____
_____

➢ You rear them in the _____ of the Lord – mild, kind, yet earnest reproof, cautionary advice or warning. When you are _____ a child you are giving them counsel against something that should be avoided because it is dangerous. Something that will take them off the course of Christian ethics.

A Father's Good Practices

- Be an _____ not a dictator

- Be a _____

- Be a _____

- Be a _____ and coach

- Be a _____ (a caring one)

- Be _____

- Be _____

- Be an _____

- Be a spiritual _____

Stewardship to Parents

First Concept – loving my parents

When we are in our parents' house, it is critical to show_____. This is important because of the law of _____ and_____. You are actually setting yourself up for a future harvest on the seeds you have sown into their lives.

This particular commandment has a _____ that many need to recognize. If your life is not going well research the _____ you left in your parents' home. If you are still having trouble in life after so many years of _____ you might want to go back and _____ for some things. Living long on the earth comes by good_____. When you do good to others, good comes back to you.

Second Concept – leaving my parents

The exhortation

When a man finds a wife, the Word says, he finds a _____ thing and obtains _____ from the Lord.

But in order for that favor to flourish, he must _____his parents' house to _____a house for his_____.

This new relationship now requires an adjustment in lifestyle. It requires a new set of priorities.

- She now becomes the _____of his life.

- She must have first place with his_____.

- She must have first place with his_____.

- She must have first place with his_____.

- She must have first place with his_____.

Third Concept – loving my parents

The exhortation

- The Word is very clear that families are _____ for their _____parents when age has overtaken them and assistance is_____.

- Paul says to be careful for those who would _____and exploit using _____to tap into their children's pocketbooks.

Fourth and Final Concept – Loving My God

The first and greatest _____is to love God with all your _____and _____and_____. Jesus says to connect with God with your _____being. He is to be the _____of your heart; He is to be the object of _____for your soul; He is the central _____that dominates your mind. From this description we are to be consumed with His presence. The way it is described is like an_____. But this addiction is the cornerstone of life itself. Everything we are, everything we have all comes from this same_____. It all comes from God. Let's look at the beginning of this love relationship in the book of Genesis.

Why is it crucial for every man to have a relationship with God?

It is crucial to have a relationship with God because of the law of _____. Whatever it took to start life is necessary to _____life. Whatever it takes to create a thing is needed to sustain a thing.

NOTES

Man cannot live his best life _____ from the One who created him.

- God made man's _____.

- God gave birth to man's _____.

- God _____ with man

- God _____ with man

- God _____ faith to man

- God _____ shelter, support, sustenance, and a spouse for man.

What does the love of God look like?

- He made the man a living_____.

- He made him a _____ in the Garden of Eden.

- He made him a _____ over the Garden.

- He made him _____ for obeying one law.

- He made him a _____ for companionship.

- He made him in His own _____ and _____.

- He made him to have _____ over all the earth.

- He made him b_____, _____l, and productive.

What a love story!

When we function as faithful Stewards, we are showing our love for Him.

- My _____ of being fruitful, multiplying, and replenishing the earth is all made possible through my _____ with Him.

The Steward's Connection

- Just like in Matthew, Jesus repeats it in John. _____ yourself in God.

- With this _____ that we have in Him it is impossible not to be fruitful.

- **The key to good Stewardship is staying connected.**

- That is what that _____ in the Garden of Eden was all about.

- Satan was trying to _____ and _____ Adam and Eve from their _____.

- The same occurred with _____ when _____ accused him of not really loving God with all his heart, but just for what he could get from God.

- It was all about the _____, nothing more – nothing less.

To disconnect you from your source is the enemy's strategy. Brothers, the key to our life and Stewardship is our connection with God.

Connection is the key to thriving as a Steward.

- Connection is the **key to** _____ – made in His image and likeness

- Connection is the **key to** _____ – given authority to rule

- Connection is the **key to** _____ – bear fruit

- Connection is the **key to** _____ – mentored for elevated faith

- Connection is the **key to** _____ – highest lifestyle possible

- Connection is the **key to** _____ – power to multiply

The key to elevation, promotion, and destiny is staying connected to my source as I carry out my Stewardship.

- Stay connected through the _____ – hearing and confessing

- Stay connected through _____ – the sacrifice of praise

- Stay connected through _____ for Him – service

- Stay connected through you're _____ – shall be witnesses unto God

NOTES

NOTES

- Stay connected through _____ on the Lord – church assembly

- Stay connected through _____ – prayer ministry, the watchman

Men Of Valor and Excellence (MOVE),

Stand on your post as a good steward, stay in faith, stay connected, stay submitted and you will experience satisfaction and fulfilment at its highest level as you complete your God given purpose.

Don't stop until you have fulfilled your assignment!

MOVE Men I call you blessed prosperous and highly favored.

Dr. Fred L. Hodge Jr.

Founder

Don't stop until you have fulfilled your assignment!

MOVE Men I call you blessed prosperous and highly favored.

Dr. Fred L. Hodge Jr.,

MOVE - Men of Valor and Excellence, Founder

Sr. Pastor, Living Praise Christian Center

Chatsworth & Palmdale Locations

ABOUT THE AUTHOR

Dr. Fred L. Hodge

Dr. Fred L. Hodge is the Founder of Living Praise Christian Church in Southern California along with his wife Linda Hodge. This dynamic couple have cultivated and developed a cutting-edge church with multiple locations. The North location is in the Antelope Valley and the South location is in the San Fernando Valley.

Fred and Linda have celebrated 34 years of marriage and 40 years in ministry. He has developed tremendous knowledge and insight in cultivating people for success. Although Dr. Hodge has experienced divorce in his past, he chose not to allow condemnation to derail his life but instead became better, not bitter and mastered the art of choosing wisely. He is a transformation speaker. His messages provoke males and females, singles, and married couples to live their best life now as they pursue a better life for their future.

Dr. Hodge is known for his practical approach to sharing the principles of personal development. He helps people reach their goals for a higher quality of life. Through his coaching and mentoring, many have been elevated to "next level" living in their pursuit of abundant life.

www.ingramcontent.com/pod-product-compliance
Lightning Source LLC
LaVergne TN
LVHW081319060426
835509LV00015B/1583